BRAIN SURGERY

for beginners

AND OTHER MAJOR OPERATIONS FOR MINORS

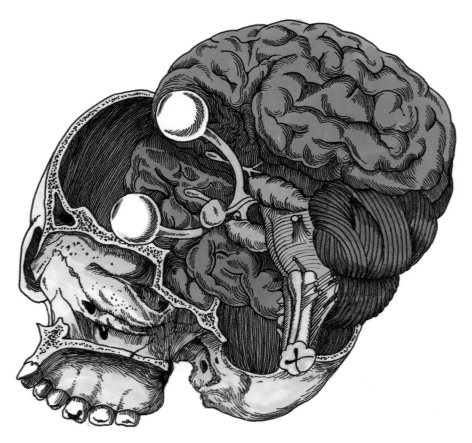

DESIGNED AND ILLUSTRATED BY
DAVID WEST
WRITTEN BY
STEVE PARKER

THE MILLBROOK PRESS

BROOKFIELD, CONNECTICUT

Created by
NW Books
28 Percy Street
London W1P 9FF

First published in 1993 in Great Britain by
Simon & Schuster Young Books
Hemel Hempstead

First published in 1995 in the United States
by The Millbrook Press
2 Old New Milford Road
Brookfield, Connecticut 06804

Library of Congress
Cataloging-in-
Publication Data
Parker, Steve.
Brain surgery for beginners and other minor
operations for minors / by Steve Parker:
designed and illustrated by David West.
p. cm.
Includes index.
ISBN 1-56294-604-8 (lib.bdg.)
     1-56294-895-4 (pbk.)
1. Brain – Juvenile literature.
2. Neurophysiology – Juvenile literature.
[1. Brain] I. West, David, ill. II. Title.
QP361.5.P37 1995
612–dc20   94–36636
                              CIP AC

For Meryl, who has a
small brain but a big
heart – SP.

For Jamie and
Oliver, who will not
eat their greens –
DW.

CONTENTS

INTRODUCTION

The human body is the most amazing living machine. *(Yes, we know.)* It is built from billions of microscopic cells, of many different kinds. *(So true.)* The main parts, or organs, of the body are grouped into systems, each with a major function. *(Here we go again.)* The respiratory system, which obtains vital oxygen, is composed of the nose, lungs ...

HOLD IT. Most human body books say these things. But there is one body part that towers above all others. It's the brain. High on its perch in the skull, the brain controls and coordinates, thinks and reacts, predicts and remembers. It is the essence of being human. So here is a book written from the brain's point of view. It shows that modern medicine can peer into many parts of the body with wondrous machines, to see what is wrong. And surgeons can repair and replace organs with spare parts. But, in the end, BRAINS RULE. OK?

SPARE-PART SURGERY

Spare-part Frankie highlights artificial devices and machines that can help or replace body parts.

SPIES ON YOUR INSIDES

Safe rays and scopes can look into the body with the minimum of risk and discomfort.

BRAINY SAYS:
"Look for my picture throughout the book. I'll show you which areas of me are in control of the body parts illustrated on the page. Remember, whatever happens in the body, I'm in charge!"

BRAIN SURGERY THROUGH THE AGES

Aristotle of Ancient Greece, who lived 2,400 years ago, is sometimes called the "Grandfather of Science." He had one of the greatest thinking brains of all time. But he would not have agreed. He believed that the body part for thoughts, memories, intelligence and reasoning was the heart! Since those early times, people have learned so much about the brain and the body, and how they work ...

WHAT A HEADACHE
Think yourself lucky that you were not around in prehistoric times. More than 10,000 years ago, the cure for a headache was a hole in the head!

Fossil-hunters have discovered the preserved bones of Neanderthal "cave people" from the Stone Age. Some of their skulls have holes in them. It seems as if the holes were made on purpose, probably hacked and chipped out with a stone axe or rock knife. The process is called trephining or trepanning. We know that the holes were made while the owners of the skulls were still alive, because some of the gaps in the skulls have partly grown over, as the poor victims lived on and their wounds tried to heal!

HOLES IN THE HEAD
Why did these people carry out trephining? Possibly the well-meaning hole-makers were trying to cure their patients of very bad headaches. Or the holes were made to let out evil spirits from the heads of people they thought were possessed or mad. Whatever the reason, these skulls are the best evidence we have for the very first brain surgeons.

Incredibly, trephining did not fade out with the Stone Age. It was still being done in the Middle Ages, using metal drills to make much cleaner, neater holes.

MAKING MUMMIES

By 4,500 years ago, the Ancient Egyptians had learned to preserve bodies with embalming fluids and spices. Their idea was to ensure that the body stayed in good shape for a long time. Then the soul, which

left its body at death, would have somewhere to return and stay, far in the future.

We call these preserved bodies "mummies." The process included removing the brain in pieces through the nose, and taking out the lungs, guts and other inner parts through a slit in the side of the body. Sometimes these organs, especially the heart, were kept in special jars of their own. The main body was treated with salts, spices, herbs and special fluids. Some of the bodies were wrapped in cloth bandages. The preservation was so good that some mummies are still around today. Those Egyptians certainly knew the inner structure, or anatomy, of the body. But what can you expect from people who worshipped cats?

THE BEGINNINGS OF MEDICINE

Like Aristotle, Hippocrates of Ancient Greece lived about 2,400 years ago. He was not impressed by some of the doctors of his time. They kept no medical records of their patients. They gave whatever treatment they liked. Often they said what the illness was, and advised a treatment, without even seeing the patient! Some of their drugs and surgical methods were so dangerous that they killed, not cured.

Hippocrates was horrified at all this. Carefully he studied how the body worked, and devised a set of guidelines for good doctors to follow. They included talking to patients, examining and testing them to identify the problem, and giving treatments for sensible reasons. Doctors should also keep records of what happened, so that they knew which treatments worked best. Hippocrates also knew that the body had great powers of self-healing, and that sometimes the best thing to do was – nothing. Today's doctors still follow his main guidelines, and this Ancient Greek is sometimes called the "Father of Medicine."

BLOOD AND GUTS

The next great step in learning about the brain and body came in Roman times. Claudius Galen lived about 2,100 years ago. He was a physician (doctor) in Rome, and attended the gladiators and slaves who fought wild animals and each other, in the Colosseum. The traditions of the time did not allow Galen to dissect, or cut open, human bodies for study. But he saw plenty of innards after the gladiator fights, and he also dissected and examined wild animals. Unlike Aristotle, Galen believed that the brain somehow controlled the body and that it was the site of the mind. But he had several weird ideas. He thought that breathing drew an invisible natural spirit, which he called *pneuma*, into the lungs and then to the heart. Here the pneuma mixed with blood containing part-digested food. The resulting mixture seeped up and down the body.

As you read this book, you will find out how wrong he was! Despite these and other mistaken ideas, Galen wrote many marvellous books about anatomy (body structure). His influence lasted for hundreds of years.

WORLD MEDICINE
In ancient times, people in many parts of the world made advances in anatomy, and in its twin science, physiology – how the body works. This knowledge helped in their medical work. The Ancient Chinese could do eye operations, take out gall stones from the liver, and make gold false teeth. In the Middle Ages in India, surgeons did operations such as removing lumps and bumps, and they used many types of herbs and minerals to cure illness. So did the medieval Arab peoples. The Arabs also revived and kept going the great anatomy books of Galen and others.

THE RENAISSANCE
From about 1300, the Renaissance period began in Europe. There was a "rebirth" in arts and sciences. One of the sciences was anatomy. Italian all-round genius Leonardo da Vinci (1452-1519) drew wonderful illustrations of bones, muscles and other body parts (as well as being a great artist, engineer, inventor, etc). Andreas Vesalius (1514-1564), who came from Brussels but worked in Italy, wrote and drew his great book *On the Structure of the Human Body* (1543). This was a landmark in the study of the body. Vesalius did his own dissections of animals, and also of human criminals.

Cutting open people, apart from the occasional criminal, was still frowned on – even after they had died. The work of Vesalius began the modern age of anatomy.

THE BLOOD GOES ROUND

Another great advance came in 1628. English physician William Harvey (1578-1657) wrote a small book called *On the Motion of the Heart and Blood*. It showed for the first time that blood went round and round the body, pumped by the heart. Before Harvey's time, people had all kinds of strange ideas about blood. They thought that it burned to warm the body, or that it evaporated as a vapor into the air.

After Harvey, there was rapid progress in anatomy, physiology and medicine. In 1846 in Massachusetts, William Morton (1819-1868) was the first to use an anesthetic during an operation, to "put the patient to sleep."

Previously, patients had to be held down, knocked out or drunk to the world. Louis Pasteur (1822-1895) of France used his skills with the microscope to identify germs. He suggested that some diseases might be caused by germs getting into the body. English surgeon Joseph Lister (1827-1912) developed the use of antiseptics during surgery, to kill germs. Before this, surgeons saw no need to wash their hands before cutting open their patients. No wonder so many died.

MODERN BRAIN SURGERY

In 1879 in Glasgow, Scotland, William Macewen (1848-1924) began the modern era of brain surgery. He operated to remove a blood clot from the brain of a patient. Surgeons were soon carrying out all kinds of brain operations. Their work showed that an illness or tumor (growth) in a certain part of the brain usually caused the same types of problems in each patient. Such problems included memory loss, changed personality, blindness, numbness and paralysis. Gradually the evidence was pieced together to show that each part of the brain has its own jobs, as you will read in this book. Modern brain surgery is incredibly complicated and delicate, and our knowledge continues to grow. If those Stone Age brain surgeons could come back today, what would they say?

CHAPTER ONE

The MAIN BRAIN

Have you got a brain? Good. So use it to understand and remember the first chapter of our book. This shows what the brain looks like, inside and out. It describes the many marvellous jobs that the brain can do, and shows how the brain is the control center for all body processes. Don't forget that you will be tested on all this at the end!

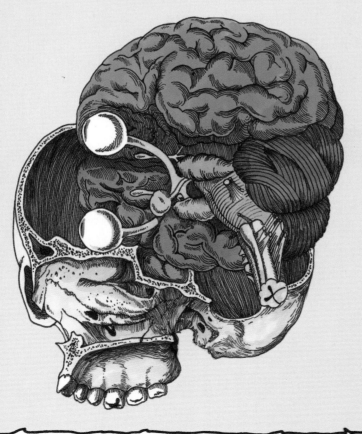

THE BITS OF THE BRAIN

The top half of your head is filled with a large lump of pinkish-gray, wrinkled looking substance, that feels like a mixture of pudding and jelly. But don't worry. All brains are like this. The human brain is the most amazing bio-computer. It can think, remember, predict, solve, create, invent, control and coordinate.

BRAIN POWER

Are you smarter than a rabbit? Almost certainly. Your brain is much bigger than the rabbit's brain. Are you smarter than a sperm whale? Again, almost certainly, even though this huge beast's brain is five times bigger than your own. Intelligence is not just a matter of brain size. It depends on the relative sizes of the brain parts, and how they are connected. The cortex, the wrinkly gray part, is huge in the human brain. This is where intelligence, thinking and complicated behavior are based.

SPIES ON YOUR INSIDES

The CAT (computerized axial tomography) scanner pictures a "slice" of the brain, with no discomfort or risk. It beams weak X-rays through the head and displays the results on a computer TV screen.

Computer

CORTEX
The outer gray part, where thinking takes place, is shown on pages 16-17.

X-rays beamed from all angles as camera goes around head.

CEREBRAL HEMISPHERES
These are the bulging, wrinkly parts. They have gray cortex on the outside, and white nerves inside.

CORPUS CALLOSUM
This long bundle of nerves links the two halves of the brain, so the right hand knows what the left hand is doing.

THALAMUS
An egg-shaped area that helps to process and recognize information about touch, pain, temperature, and pressure on the skin.

LIMBIC SYSTEM
Sometimes called the "emotional brain," the wishbone-shaped limbic system is involved in anger, fear, pleasure and sorrow.

HIPPOCAMPUS
Supposedly shaped like a seahorse, hence its name, the hippocampus is part of the memory system.

CEREBELLUM
This is like a mini-brain within the whole brain. It is vital for carrying out skilled, complicated movements, like doing a brain operation.

Stalk of cerebellum

PONS
This name means "bridge." The pons is a crossroads for nerves going up to the cortex, back to the cerebellum, and down to the spinal cord.

Medulla

Spinal cord

ELECTRICAL BRAINS
In 1800, Alessandro Volta of Italy invented the battery. He spent many years arguing with Luigi Galvani, who had discovered electricity while experimenting on animal nerves and brains.

THE UNDER-BRAIN

From the outside, the brain is dominated by the two huge, domed, wrinkled cerebral hemispheres. Take these away (if you dare), and the "under-parts" shown here are revealed. They are mostly involved in subconscious activities, that just "happen."

Tail of caudate nucleus

Lentiform nucleus

Caudate nucleus

I'M SOOOO HAPPY

Besides emotions (page 12), the limbic system also controls behavior that helps us to act normally. It may generate laughter and happiness, then dampen this down, so that the laughter does not get out of hand. Otherwise people might think we have gone completely crazy.

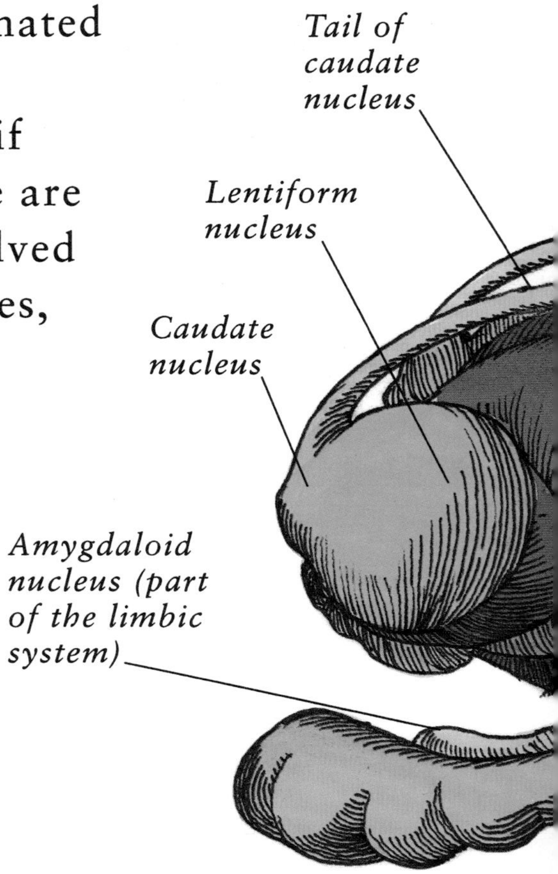

Amygdaloid nucleus (part of the limbic system)

LEFT, RIGHT
The lentiform and caudate parts shown above make up a brain area called the basal ganglia. It helps us to make almost automatic movements that we hardly ever think about, like swinging our arms when we walk.

AN ARMY AT WORK
Like soldiers on duty, the automatic brain never shirks its jobs or gets distracted. Otherwise we might forget to breathe, or our heartbeat might stop. The brain's under-parts control blood pressure and body temperature, and do dozens of other jobs.

HOT LINES THROUGH THE BRAIN

Brain parts such as the thalamus process and pass on information about touch and other senses. Usually you take little notice, for instance, if your socks press on your feet. But if something serious touches your skin, you know about it at once!

Thalamus

THE BODY'S COMPUTER

There have been many attempts at comparing the human brain to a modern computer. The computer can add up or multiply faster than we can. But can it appreciate a beautiful painting or enjoy a good book?

KNIT ONE, PURL ONE ...

It's hard to learn a complicated activity, such as riding a bicycle or knitting. Yet after a time, it's so easy. The cerebellum has taken over auto-control of the muscles.

Cerebellum

Medulla

PONS

This "bridge" (page 13) contains millions and millions of nerve fibers. Imagine a real highway bridge system with as many different crossovers and intersections!

SNORE, SNORE

The medulla is the main controller of heartbeat and breathing, including snoring! It is also the center for reactions such as sneezing and coughing.

The under-parts are almost covered by the cerebral hemispheres.

THE THINKING BRAIN

The main part of the brain that we use to think, decide and reason is the cortex – the thin gray layer on the wrinkled domes of the two cerebral hemispheres. The cortex looks the same all over. But brain research has "mapped" it to show its different parts are specialized for different jobs. We have maps on the brain!

PERSONALITY
Are you a good, kind person? Of course! The frontal lobes take part in the complex behaviors we call personality.

LEFT BRAIN, RIGHT BRAIN

In most people, the two halves of the cortex seem to have different tendencies. The right side is most involved in creative and artistic abilities such as painting, drawing, writing and playing music.

Artistic brilliance

Scientific excellence

The left side tends to take over in logical and rational thinking, as when solving mathematical sums, doing scientific experiments, playing chess and working out what to say.

SENSOR AND MOTOR

These two drawings show how we would look, if each part of our body was in proportion to the area of cortex dealing with it. One is for skin's touch, the sensory cortex. The other is for muscle movement, the motor cortex.

Motoring man   *Sensitive man*

16

MUSCLE CONTROL
The motor cortex is in overall control of the muscles, ordering them to work so that we can move.

THE INS AND OUTS
Information whizzes around the brain and body along nerves, as tiny electrical blips called nerve signals. Sensory signals come into the brain from the eyes, ears and other senses. Motor signals go out to the muscles.

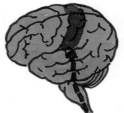

1 Signals come in from the senses.

TOUCH
The somato-sensory cortex is the "touch center." It receives information from all over our skin, about things we touch, and whether they feel hot or cold, or press hard, or cause pain.

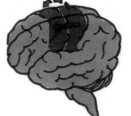

2 The brain decides what to do.

SIGHT
The visual cortex receives and processes information from the eyes. It works out shapes, colors and movements, and identifies what we see. It is the site of the "mind's eye."

3 Signals go out to the muscles.

SMELL AND TASTE
The olfactory cortex sorts out smelly signals from the nose. The gustatory cortex is part of the touch area and receives tastes.

SPIES ON YOUR INSIDES

Another scanning method for looking inside the brain is PET (positron emission tomography). The PET scan shows where the brain is busiest and most active.

HEARING
Information from our ears, in the form of nerve signals, travels to the auditory cortex. Here it is sorted out and analyzed. We can identify most sounds by comparing them with sound patterns in our memory banks. For a strange or unusual sound, we may turn the head to see what has made it.

GRAY MATTERS

When we want someone to think hard, we say, "Use your gray matter!" The gray matter is the cortex. It is composed of microscopic nerve cells, as shown here. (The inner parts of the brain are made mainly of nerve fibers, so they are white.) The millions of nerve cells connect to each other in billions of ways, forming trillions of pathways for nerve signals to follow.

SPIES ON YOUR INSIDES

The electron microscope does not use light rays, but beams of atomic particles called electrons. It can see individual body cells in amazing detail, and show how nerve cells are linked together.

PILLOWS IN THE HEAD

The cortex fits in the head because it is so folded and wrinkly. Smoothed out, it would have the surface area of a pillowcase.

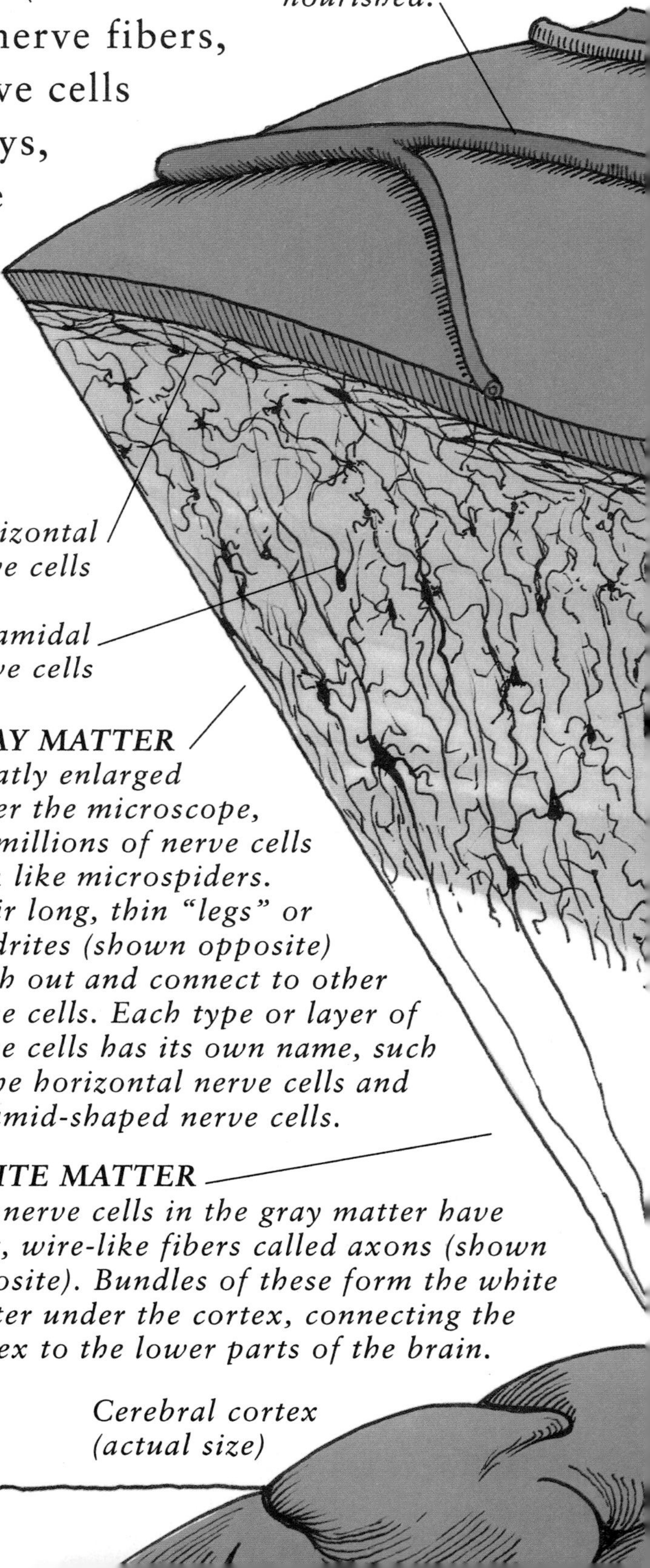

FEEDING THE BRAIN
Blood vessels bring oxygen and energy to keep the brain nourished.

Horizontal nerve cells

Pyramidal nerve cells

GRAY MATTER
Greatly enlarged under the microscope, the millions of nerve cells look like microspiders. Their long, thin "legs" or dendrites (shown opposite) reach out and connect to other nerve cells. Each type or layer of nerve cells has its own name, such as the horizontal nerve cells and pyramid-shaped nerve cells.

WHITE MATTER
The nerve cells in the gray matter have long, wire-like fibers called axons (shown opposite). Bundles of these form the white matter under the cortex, connecting the cortex to the lower parts of the brain.

Cerebral cortex (actual size)

CUSHION IN THE HEAD

On the outside of the brain, between it and the inside of the skull, are three thin coverings called the meninges. From the outside in, they are the dura mater, arachnoid and pia mater. They wrap around the brain like soft cushions, protecting it from jolts and knocks on the head.

NERVE CELLS AND SIGNALS

A single nerve cell has a rounded part called the cell body. From this extend several thin, spidery parts called dendrites, and one thicker, wire-like part, the axon. The tips of the dendrites pick up nerve signals from other nerve cells. They send the signals along the axon, to dendrites of more nerve cells.

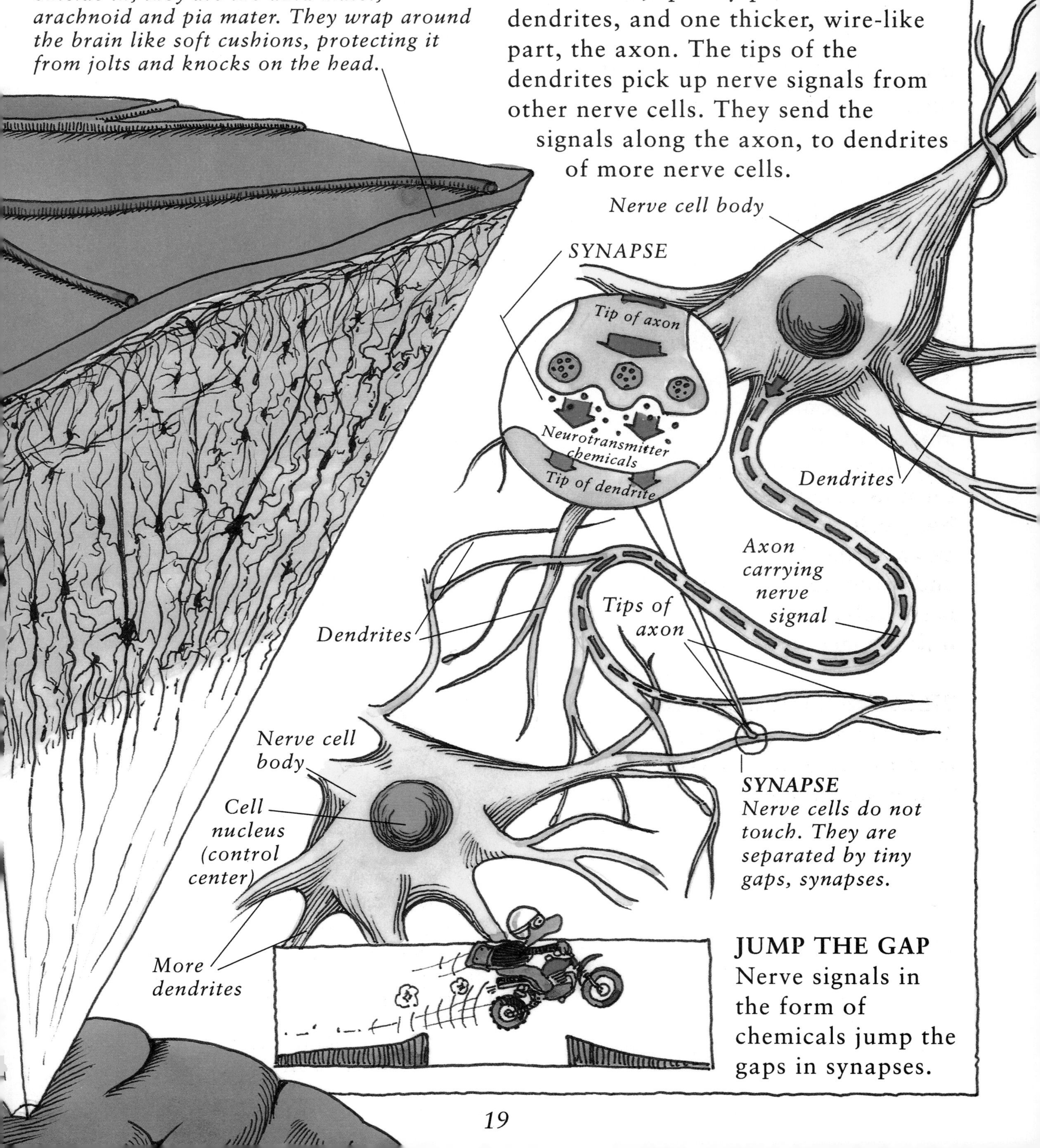

Nerve cell body

SYNAPSE

Tip of axon

Neurotransmitter chemicals

Tip of dendrite

Dendrites

Dendrites

Tips of axon

Axon carrying nerve signal

Nerve cell body

Cell nucleus (control center)

SYNAPSE
Nerve cells do not touch. They are separated by tiny gaps, synapses.

More dendrites

JUMP THE GAP
Nerve signals in the form of chemicals jump the gaps in synapses.

19

WIRES TO THE BRAIN

The brain does not sit by itself, alone in the skull. It has two types of nerve connections to its body. One is the 12 pairs of cranial nerves. These sprout from the brain and link it directly to important parts such as the eyes, nose, ears and jaws. The second type is the spinal cord, which goes through the neck to the body (page 22).

Suture

THE BRAINCASE
The upper rounded part of the skull is the cranium. It is made of eight curved bones. These are fixed firmly together at wiggly-line joints known as sutures, to form a strong, rigid, protective case for the brain.

SPIES ON YOUR INSIDES

Did you know that your brain contains sloshy liquid? It is called cerebrospinal fluid. It fills chambers inside the brain called ventricles, and helps to nourish the inner brain parts. The fluid shows up clearly on another type of scan, the MRI (magnetic resonance imaging) scan.

FROM BELOW
The main drawing shows the brain taken out of its skull, and viewed from the side and below.

HOLEY SKULL (1)
The skull bones in the face have holes in them, called sinuses. These join to the inside of the nose and are filled with air. They help to lighten the skull's weight, and work as vibration chambers for the voice.

THE SKULL JIGSAW
The whole skull is an intricate 3-D jigsaw of 28 different bones. The smallest are the three tiny bones deep inside each ear.

FROM THE EYES
The optic nerve is cranial nerve number two. It carries sensory signals from the eyes, about what we see. It contains over one million axons, or nerve fibers.

Eyeball

FROM THE NOSE
The olfactory nerve is cranial nerve number one. It brings information from the nose, about what we smell. The wide part is called the olfactory bulb, and the thinner part leading to the underside of the brain is the olfactory tract.

Olfactory bulb

Olfactory tract

THE MASTER GLAND
No bigger than a baked bean, the pituitary gland is the master controller of the body's hormone system (page 59). It connects to the brain by the small pituitary stalk.

THE FACE
Cranial nerve number five is the trigeminal. It brings sensory signals from the face skin and inside the mouth and nose, about touch. It also takes motor signals to the chewing muscles.

Spinal cord

Hole in base of skull for spinal cord

SPARE-PART SURGERY

If a skull bone breaks, it can be replaced with a curved metal plate.

HOLEY SKULL (2)
This underside view shows the various holes in the skull, where the nerves come out.

WHAT A NERVE!

The brain's connection with the spinal cord means that it is wired into the main nerve network. This network branches from the spinal cord out through the entire body, from scalp to toes. The brain, spinal cord and nerves are together called the nervous system.

Spinal cord

MAIN NERVE
About 18 inches long, and thick as a thumb, the spinal cord is the body's main bundle of nerves.

PROTECTING THE CORD
The row of backbones, or vertebrae, form a protective tunnel for the spinal cord. They prevent it from getting knocked or kinked.

Brain

Spinal cord

Ulnar, medial and radial nerves in arm

NERVE ROOTS
These are the junctions between the spinal cord and the major nerves branching off into the body.

Thoracic nerves in chest

NERVES
Dozens of nerves branch from the spinal cord like pieces of thin gray rope. Some are sensory, carrying signals to the brain. Others are motor, taking signals from brain to muscles. Still others are both sensory and motor.

Visceral nerves in abdomen

Sciatic and femoral nerves in leg

OOW!
A pinch sends signals up to the spinal cord, and back to muscles – a reflex reaction.

SPEEDY SIGNALS
Nerve signals flash around faster than an express train!

CHAPTER TWO

The
AUTO-BRAIN

The brain is terribly busy and bossy. Every second, it sends out orders to body parts such as the heart, lungs and guts, telling them to keep beating, breathing and squirming. We do not have to remember to do all these automatic actions. Just as well, otherwise we would never have time to do other things, such as read this next chapter ...

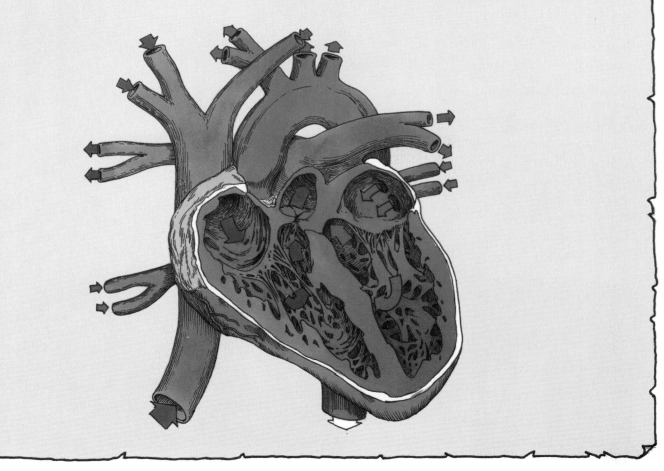

BRAIN BREATHS

Like any living thing, the brain needs oxygen. After a few minutes without oxygen, it would start to fade and die – and we wouldn't want that.

Oxygen is an invisible gas that makes up one-fifth of the air around the body. But it cannot seep through the skull bones, straight into the brain. It must first go down the windpipe into the lungs, then into the blood, and finally to the brain.

Rib breathing muscles

HIC, PUFF, PANT

Sometimes the smooth in-out movements of breathing are interrupted. Hiccups are uncontrolled in-breaths, usually when the main breathing muscle, the diaphragm, gets stretched by a too-full stomach just below it. When the body is very active, its muscles need more oxygen, so the breathing gets faster and we pant.

TUBE-CLEANING
Tiny hairs, cilia, and slimy mucus line the breathing tubes. The mucus traps dust and germs; the cilia wave to sweep it upward, to be swallowed.

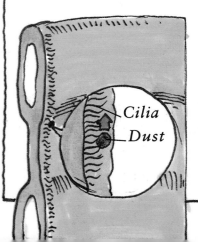

Cilia
Dust

SPIES ON YOUR INSIDES

Modern X-ray machines can do wondrous things, especially when helped by computers. In the bronchoscopy, the breathing tubes are lined with a special fluid that shows up on the X-ray picture. A computer can color the picture to make it easier to see the details.

RIBS
These long, springy bones form a protective cage for the delicate heart and lungs. They are hinged so that they move up and down when breathing.

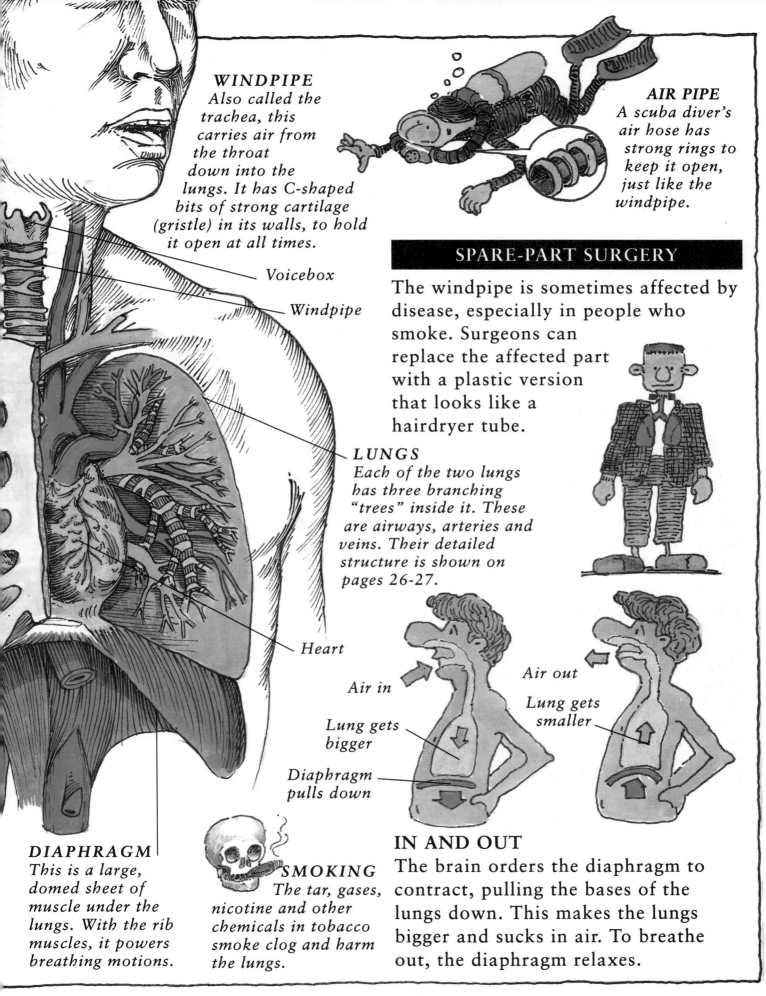

WINDPIPE
Also called the trachea, this carries air from the throat down into the lungs. It has C-shaped bits of strong cartilage (gristle) in its walls, to hold it open at all times.

Voicebox

Windpipe

AIR PIPE
A scuba diver's air hose has strong rings to keep it open, just like the windpipe.

SPARE-PART SURGERY

The windpipe is sometimes affected by disease, especially in people who smoke. Surgeons can replace the affected part with a plastic version that looks like a hairdryer tube.

LUNGS
Each of the two lungs has three branching "trees" inside it. These are airways, arteries and veins. Their detailed structure is shown on pages 26-27.

Heart

Air in

Lung gets bigger

Diaphragm pulls down

Air out

Lung gets smaller

DIAPHRAGM
This is a large, domed sheet of muscle under the lungs. With the rib muscles, it powers breathing motions.

SMOKING
The tar, gases, nicotine and other chemicals in tobacco smoke clog and harm the lungs.

IN AND OUT
The brain orders the diaphragm to contract, pulling the bases of the lungs down. This makes the lungs bigger and sucks in air. To breathe out, the diaphragm relaxes.

IN THE LUNGS

Deep in the lungs, something stirs. It is air, gently wafting in and out with each breath. The lungs' main air pipes, the bronchi, branch many times until they form hair-thin tubes, terminal bronchioles. These end in grape-like bunches of air bubbles, called alveoli. There are over 300 million alveoli in each lung. It is here that oxygen passes into the blood.

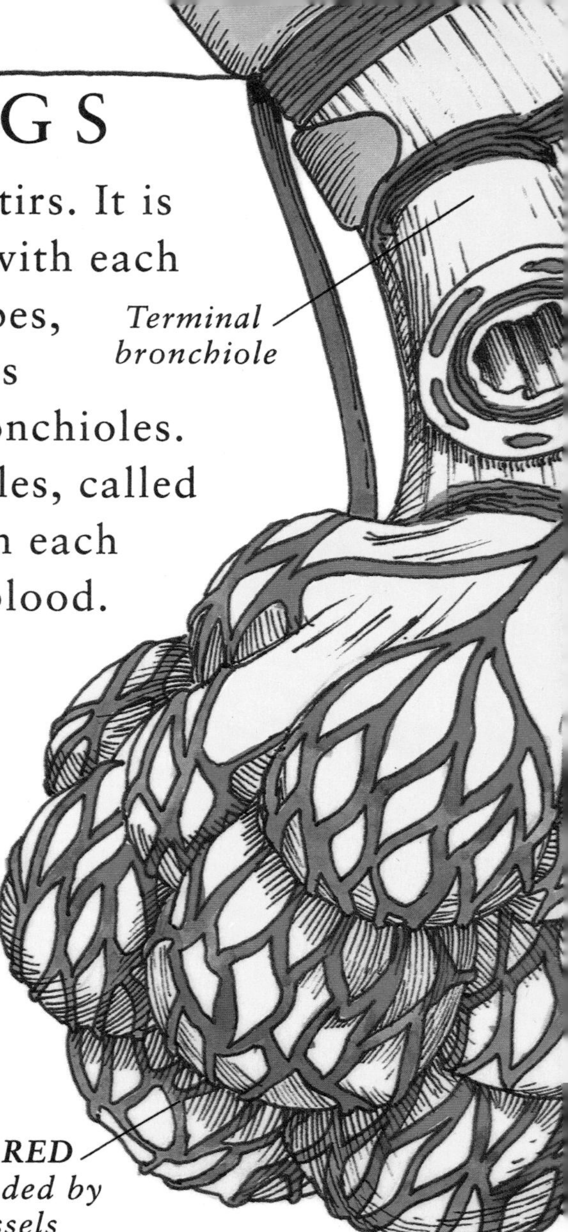

Terminal bronchiole

SLOW AND FAST

The brain constantly adjusts the breathing rate, according to the body's activity and oxygen needs. When we rest or sleep, the breathing rate is 15-20 breaths each minute. After running a race, it goes up to over 60 breaths each minute.

CHANGED AIR

Breathed-in air is about one-fifth oxygen, O_2. Coming back out, this proportion has changed to one-sixth. The difference is made up by carbon dioxide, CO_2, one of the body's waste products. Nitrogen, which makes up four-fifths of air, stays unchanged.

BLUE TO RED

Each alveolus air-bubble is surrounded by a network of microscopic blood vessels known as capillaries. Blue oxygen-poor blood flows into the capillaries. Here it picks up oxygen from the air inside the alveolus (as shown opposite), and turns into bright red, oxygen-rich blood.

Bronchus

Alveoli

AIRWAY TREE

The bronchi branch 15 or 20 times to form the tiny bronchioles, with alveoli at their tips.

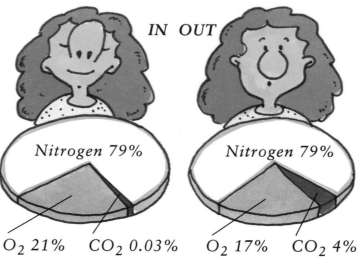

IN OUT

Nitrogen 79% | Nitrogen 79%

O_2 21% CO_2 0.03% O_2 17% CO_2 4%

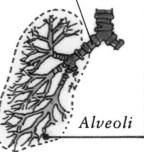

BLOOD IN
Stale blue blood arrives at the alveoli along tiny arteries called arterioles.

BLOOD OUT
Refreshed red blood leaves the capillaries around the alveoli along miniature veins, venules.

DEEP-DIVING MOUSE
Deep-sea divers must breathe a special mixture of gases, including helium, due to the great water pressure. But breathing helium makes their voices sound like Mickey Mouse!

INSIDE AN ALVEOLUS
The wall of an alveolus is only one cell thick – which is extremely thin! The wall of the blood capillary is only one cell thin, too. So oxygen in the air inside the alveolus has hardly any distance to go, to get into the blood.

THE NON-STOP SWOP
Swopping the oxygen coming from the air to the blood, for the carbon dioxide going from the blood to the air, is gas exchange.

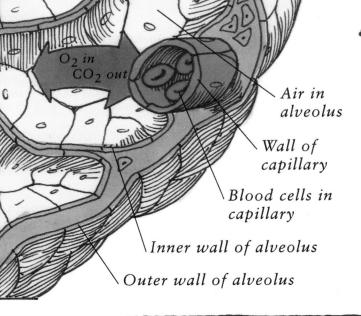

O_2 in
CO_2 out

Air in alveolus

Wall of capillary

Blood cells in capillary

Inner wall of alveolus

Outer wall of alveolus

LARGE AS OUR LUNGS
If a surgeon could iron all the alveoli flat, they would cover a huge surface, large as a tennis court. That's a big area for gas exchange!

THE TALKING BRAIN

People open their mouths and speak without thinking. They say the most stupid things! Actually, even the simplest "Hello there!" needs a great deal of brain power. The brain assesses the situation, chooses the right words from the memory banks, puts them in the correct order, and sends nerve signals to dozens of muscles in the neck, throat and mouth, so that the words come out clearly.

AT THE TOP OF THE VOICE

The loudness or volume of sound is measured in decibels, dB. A quiet whisper is 30 dB. Ordinary talking is 60 dB. Normal cheering and shouting is 80 dB. The loudest ever human scream was 128 dB, which is about the same as a jackhammer!

LOTS OF WIND

The voice works like a reed instrument such as the clarinet.

3 Sound out

1 Air from lungs

1 Air from lungs

2 Vocal cords vibrate

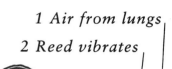

2 Reed vibrates

FROM BRAIN TO VOICEBOX

Wernicke's area selects and orders the words. Broca's area prepares instructions for voicebox, neck and mouth movements. The motor cortex sends out the nerve signals.

Wernicke's area
Broca's area
Motor signals

Sound from nose and mouth

Vocal cords vibrate

Air up from lungs

SPARE-PART SURGERY

Rarely, the voicebox gets diseased. Surgeons can replace it with a plastic version, or move pieces of skin and other body parts to help create a new one. It sounds strange, but better than no voice at all.

INSIDE THE VOICEBOX

Inside the neck, nine curved plates of cartilage (gristle) form the voicebox, or larynx. This view shows the inside of the voicebox from the rear, looking forward. Two pearly-white strips, the vocal cords, stick out from its sides. More than a dozen muscles move and stretch the cords, to vary vocal sounds.

Hyoid bone

EPIGLOTTIS
This moveable flap tilts over the entrance to the windpipe when swallowing, to prevent food getting in.

Thyroid cartilage

NECK BUMP
The thyroid cartilage on the front of the voicebox sticks out slightly, as the "Adam's apple."

Hoop of cartilage in windpipe wall

TOGETHERNESS
To talk, the voicebox muscles pull the cords close together. They rattle and vibrate as air passes between them. For normal breathing, the cords are apart.

Together for speech

Apart for breathing

VOCAL CORDS
To speak in a deep, low voice, the brain orders the voicebox muscles to bring the vocal cords almost together, but not to stretch them. To make higher, squeakier sounds, the cords stretch longer and tighter.

Corniculate cartilage

SPIES ON YOUR INSIDES

The telescope-type device called a laryngoscope looks down into the throat to see the vocal cords.

THE RED STUFF

No matter how frightened the brain is, it never faints at the sight of blood, because blood brings life. Blood carries vital oxygen, energy in the form of blood sugars, nourishing nutrients for growth and repair, the chemical messengers called hormones, and dozens of other essential substances. So smile and be thankful for this red, endlessly flowing river of life.

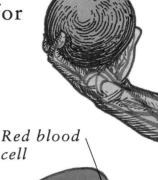

A heavy ball

BLOOD GROUPS

All blood is not the same. Each body has its own blood group. Doctors found this when they tried transfusing blood (opposite), and often failed. One set of blood groups is A, B, AB or O. Another is Rh positive or negative, named because it was discovered in rhesus monkeys.

Red blood cell

Platelet

White blood cell

SELF-SEALING SYSTEM

If a blood vessel springs a small leak, it soon seals and mends itself, by forming a sticky scab. Some car radiators do the same (with water).

Injury causes leak

BLOOD CELLS
Red cells carry oxygen. White cells fight germs. Platelets help blood to clot.

Scab seals leak

THREE TUBES FOR BLOOD

Big arteries carry blood from the heart. They divide into capillaries, which are tiny. These join into veins, and return blood to the heart.

Capillary

Main artery

Small artery

Arteriole

O_2 *and nutrients out*

CO_2 *and wastes in*

CAROTID ARTERY
This tube brings blood to the face, head and brain.

Subclavian artery and vein

Heart

Aorta (main artery)

Vena cava (main vein)

Iliac artery

Iliac vein

Femoral artery

Femoral vein

Saphenous vein

Tibial artery

Pedal arteries and veins

Venule

JUGULAR VEIN
It takes head and brain blood back to the heart.

SPARE-PART SURGERY

Been to the blood bank recently? Most people can safely give, or donate, a small amount of blood. It is treated and put in cold storage. It can be transfused into a person who is injured or ill and needs extra blood.

BODY-WIDE BLOOD

The body's eight or nine pints of blood flow round a network of arteries, capillaries and veins, called the circulatory system. The regular pumping of the heart (page 32) keeps blood on the move.

SPIES ON YOUR INSIDES

The angiogram is another type of X-ray picture. It displays blood vessels that have been injected with a special chemical, which shows up and reveals any blocks or leaks in the tubes.

Main vein

LUB-DUP, LUB-DUP

... lub-dup says the heart in the chest. The brain, far above, can just hear its comforting pumping, and feel the surges of blood with each beat. The heart is so vital, yet surgeons can operate on it by replacing it for a time with a mechanical pump.

ONE
Blood flows into atria.

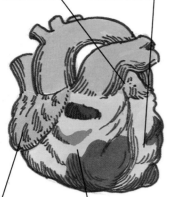

Atrium *Ventricle*

Atrium *Ventricle*

BASIC DESIGN
The heart has two upper atria, and two lower ventricles.

COMINGS AND GOINGS

From the right ventricle, stale blood goes to the lungs, for more supplies of oxygen. Refreshed, it comes back to the left atrium. It passes into the left ventricle, and is pumped all around the body, to supply every tiny bit with oxygen. Then the blood returns, stale and worn out, to the right atrium. It flows through to the right ventricle, which is where it started. And off it goes again.

From head along right jugular vein

From arm along right subclavian vein

To right lung along right pulmonary artery

MUSCLE WALL
The walls of the heart are made from thick muscle, called cardiac muscle or myocardium.

SPARE-PART SURGERY

Surgeons can replace diseased heart valves with mechanical versions. They can also connect an electronic pace-maker to keep the beats regular.

RED VEINS?
Veins bring blood back to the heart. Blood returning from the lungs along these pulmonary veins is rich in oxygen and bright red. So these veins carry red blood.

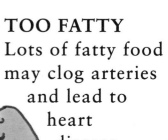

TOO FATTY
Lots of fatty food may clog arteries and lead to heart disease.

TWO
Blood flows to ventricles.

THREE
Ventricles pump hard.

FOUR
Blood spurts into arteries.

A HEARTBEAT

Blood flows in from veins, and through the atria to the ventricles, which pump it into the arteries.

Tiny electrical signals pass through the heart as it beats. An ECG (electro-cardiograph) displays these as wavy lines.

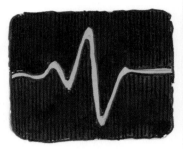

From head and left arm along brachio-cephalic vein

To head along carotid artery and to arm along subclavian artery

To left lung along left pulmonary arteries

From left lung along pulmonary veins

LEFT ATRIUM
This slack, thin-walled upper chamber receives blood oozing in from the pulmonary veins.

Mitral valve

LEFT VENTRICLE
This strong, thick-walled lower chamber provides the pumping power to send blood all around the body.

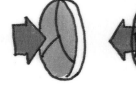

No backflow   *OK flow*

ONE-WAY FLOW
Valves in the heart make blood flow one way only.

Tricuspid valve

Vena cava (main vein)   *Right ventricle*

DEFENDING THE BRAIN

The body does its best to keep out germs and other harmful things. The skin is a strong barrier to dirt and microbes. But sometimes germs get in, breathed through the nose, or on food through the mouth. If they enter, a whole body defense system is waiting to kill, kill, kill.

Cleaned and filtered lymph fluid out

Lymph node

THE LYMPH SYSTEM
Around the body, in its own set of vessels, flows lymph. It is a pale fluid that came originally from blood. It passes through grape-sized parts called lymph nodes, or "glands," where germs are attacked.

AND SO TO BED
When we feel ill, with a high temperature and swollen lymph "glands," rest is best.

Dirty lymph fluid in, laden with germs and debris

Clusters of lymph nodes in armpit

Lymph vessels

SPLEEN HQ
The spleen is a central base for training white cells and filtering blood, especially in childhood.

Clusters of lymph nodes in groin

BATTLE IN THE BODY
It's war – not in outer space, but in inner space. White cells in blood and lymph attack germs in various ways.

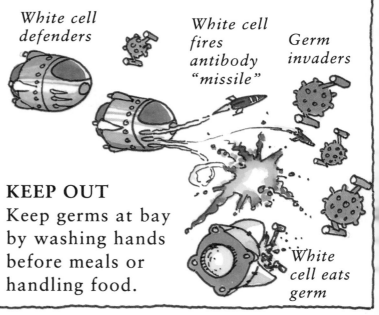

White cell defenders

White cell fires antibody "missile"

Germ invaders

KEEP OUT
Keep germs at bay by washing hands before meals or handling food.

White cell eats germ

CHAPTER THREE

The HUNGRY BRAIN

The brain is the most energy-hungry part of the body. Even the pumping heart and the busy liver do not use as much energy. A whole body system, the digestive system, is devoted to taking in food, breaking it down, absorbing it, and getting its energy and nutrients into the blood, so they can go to the brain (and to other body parts, of course).

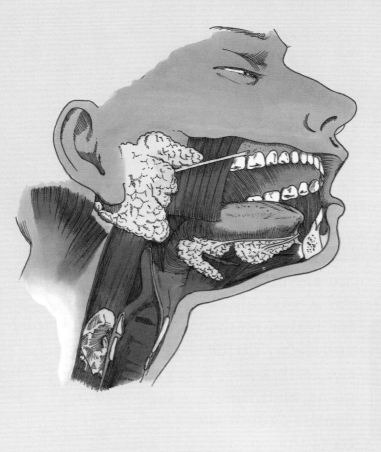

DOWN THE HATCH

Using its body's senses of eyes, and especially nose, the hungry brain soon sees and smells a yummy meal of nourishing food. It sets the mouth watering, the tongue tasting and the teeth chomping. Soon the chewed food is on its way down the hatch, swallowed into the gullet.

GULP! THAT'S EASY

Swallowing seems simple. But it uses dozens of mouth and neck muscles, controlled by the auto-brain.

TOO MUCH FOOD

Being overweight puts strain on the heart, vessels, joints and other body parts. Eat less. Exercise more!

SALIVA
Made in three pairs of salivary glands, saliva moistens food.

Parotid salivary gland

Tongue moves food back

Food in throat

Food enters top of gullet

SPIES ON YOUR INSIDES

The X-ray machine can see into our teeth and gums. Dental X-rays check for rotten teeth, and decay inside the teeth and gums, that the dentist cannot see from the outside.

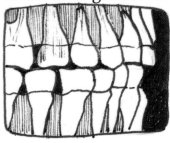

TO THE STOMACH

The gullet, or esophagus, is a muscular tube 10 inches long. It squeezes swallowed food from the throat to the stomach.

Lump of swallowed fry

Windpipe

BITE, SLICE, TEAR, RIP, CRUNCH, CHEW, CHOMP

Different teeth are designed for different jobs. The chisel-shaped incisors bite and slice. The more pointed canines tear. The broad premolars and molars crush and chew.

Left upper teeth

Left lower teeth

BABY TEETH

2 incisors 1 canine 2 molars

ADULT TEETH

Left upper teeth

Left lower teeth

2 Incisors | 2 Premolars | 3 Molars
Canine

Salivary duct

Tongue

CHEWING POWER

The temporalis and masseter muscles run from the side of the head and cheekbone, down to the lower jaw. They close the jaw with tremendous force.

Next low-fat, high-fiber fry

Front incisor tooth in jaw bone

Lower jaw bone (mandible)

Sublingual salivary gland

Submandibular salivary gland

CLEENY-WEENY TEETH

A good brushing two or three times daily, helps teeth and gums stay healthy and clean.

SPARE-PART SURGERY

The friendly local dentist can do all kinds of small spare part operations, such as putting in metal or ceramic fillings, crowns (tooth coverings) and hard plastic false teeth.

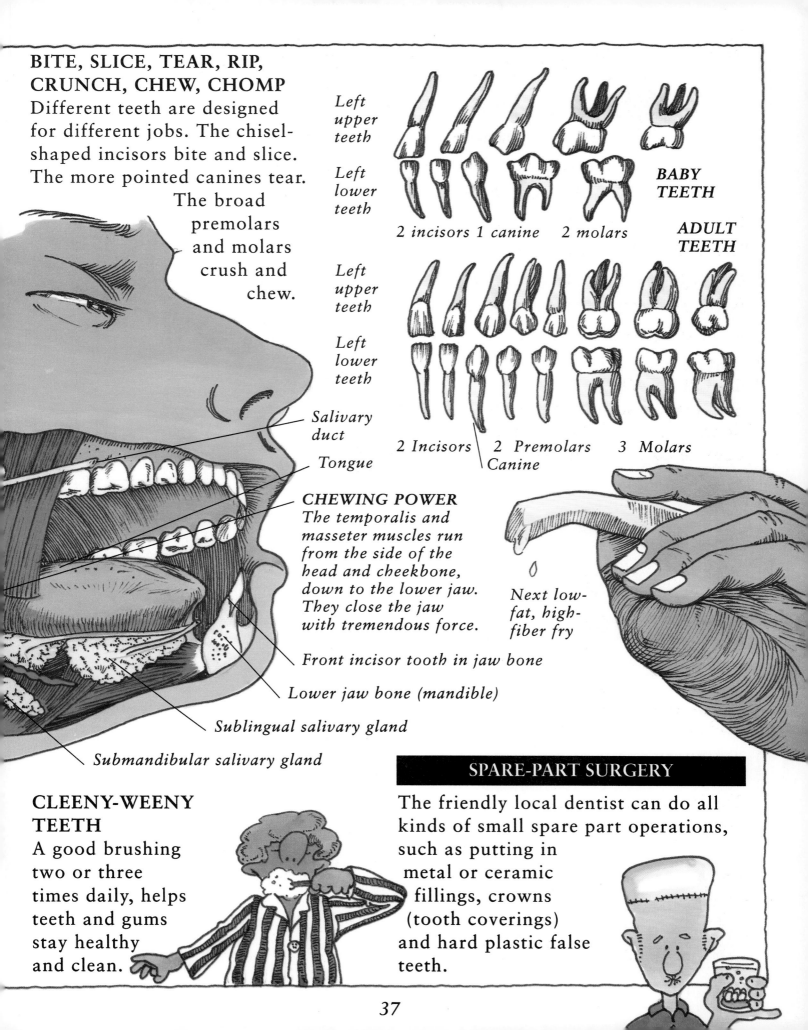

GUTS GALORE

Swallowed stuff's first stop is the stomach, which smashes it to a pulp and soaks it in digestive chemicals.

Then it sloshes along the small intestine, where the nourishing parts are absorbed into the blood. Next is the large intestine, which takes back most of the water and body minerals. The leftovers? Well, er, they ...

EXCUSE ME
Digestive processes produce gases. These can come out of the mouth, or the other end. It's natural.

... GET GOT RID OF
Semi-solid leftovers from the digestive process are stored in the rectum, near the end of the digestive system. When it is convenient, we dispose of them into the toilet.

FOOD PROCESSOR
The liver receives blood rich in nutrients from the intestine walls. It stores nutrients, and processes and changes others.

Large intestine

SPIES ON YOUR INSIDES

The gastroscope is a long, flexible tube with a light-and-viewing system at the tip. A surgeon can thread it carefully down the mouth and gullet to see the inside of the stomach or intestine.

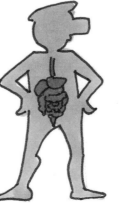

Sleeping patient

A LONG WAY
The whole length of the digestive tube, from mouth to other end, is over 26 feet.

Appendix

PUSHING FOOD

Food is pushed down the gullet by waves of contraction of the muscles in its wall. This process, peristalsis, continues through the stomach and intestines, massaging food along.

Muscles contract here

Muscles contract here

Rarely, disease affects the stomach or intestines. The affected part can be replaced by a special body opening and bag, the colostomy.

Muscular wall of stomach

Spleen

INSIDE THE STOMACH

The stomach has a tough, ridged lining covered with slimy mucus. The mucus stops the strong digestive acids and juices, which are made by gland cells in the stomach lining, from digesting the stomach itself.

Pancreas

Magnified view of stomach lining

Gland cells

Magnified view of villus

Blood and lymph vessels inside villus

SMALL INTESTINE

This is the narrowest part of the digestive tube, but the longest. Its lining looks like a furry carpet because of thousands of tiny, finger-shaped villi. They give a huge surface area for absorbing nutrients.

Outer muscle layer

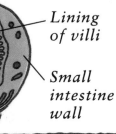

Lining of villi

Small intestine wall

Rectum

Outlet (anus)

WANT NOT?
WASTE IT!

Leftovers from digestion are one kind of body waste. There is another kind – the numerous waste chemicals that the body makes as part of its life processes. These are collected by the blood and removed by the kidneys.

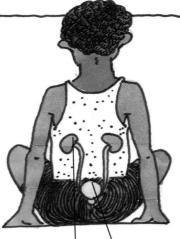

Kidney *Bladder*

THE KIDNEY
Inside the kidney is an outer part that filters the blood, and inner spaces that collect the urine.

Renal artery brings blood to kidney

Blood-filtering part

Inner space

MICROFILTERS
A kidney contains one million tiny filters, nephrons. Each one is a tangle of tubes that takes the unwanted wastes out of the blood.

Renal vein takes blood from kidney

URETER
This muscular tube carries urine from the kidney to the bladder

Nephrons

MUST GO!
The bladder is a stretchy bag that fills with urine, then expels it to the outside.

Bladder wall

SPARE-PART SURGERY

If a kidney goes wrong, its role can be replaced by a device called the renal dialysis machine. The person sits next to it, and the blood is led along tubes for filtering. A kidney transplant may be possible in some cases.

GONE
Urine flows from the bladder to the outside along the urethra.

CHAPTER FOUR

The WATCHFUL BRAIN

All the time, even as we sleep, the brain is on the alert. If it hears a strange sound, or smells danger such as smoke, it wakes us up and gets ready for action. This chapter shows how the brain gathers its information from the body's senses. There are five main senses: sight, hearing, smell, taste and touch.

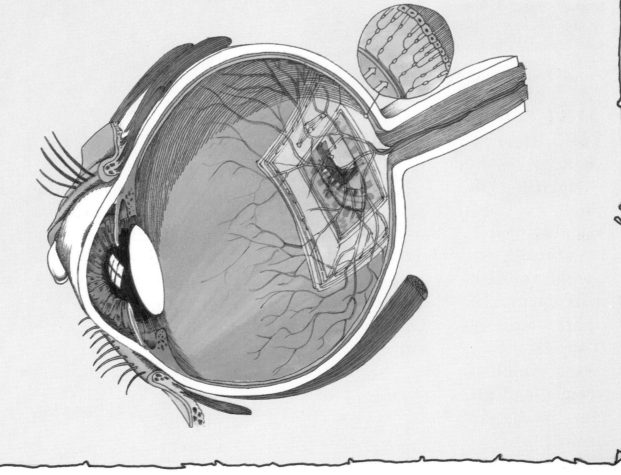

THE ALL-SEEING BRAIN

The eyes are the brain's windows on the world. Through them, the brain sees shapes, colors and movements. It identifies familiar objects, investigates strange ones, and keeps a lookout for food, drink, comfort, danger and computer games.

BRIGHT OR DIM?
No, not you – the light. The hole in the front of the eye, the pupil, gets smaller in bright light. This prevents too much light from damaging the retina. Eye color is the color of the iris.

Bright light (blue eye) *Dim light (brown eye)*

SPIES ON YOUR INSIDES

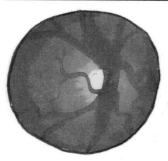

The doctor looks into the eye with a light-and-lens instrument, the ophthalmoscope. It shows the retina, blood vessels, and gives clues to the eye's health.

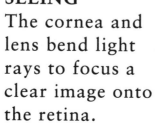

BLINKING EYES
Blinking smears tear fluid over the eye surface, to wipe off dust and germs.

SEEING
The cornea and lens bend light rays to focus a clear image onto the retina.

Eyebrow-raising muscle

Eyelid-closing muscle

Cornea
Iris
Pupil
Lens

Object

Cornea and lens

Upside down image

Nerve signals to brain

EYEBALL LAYERS

The sclera is the eye's tough outer layer. The choroid is rich in blood vessels.

Sclera

Choroid

Close-up view of retina

LANDING LIGHT

Light rays land on the retina, the eye's inner layer, It is no bigger (or thicker) than a postage stamp. Here 130 million special cells, rods and cones, detect the light rays and change their energy into nerve signals. These flash along the optic nerve to the brain.

Nerve fibers in optic nerve

Image on retina

Cross-over

CROSS EYES

The optic nerves part-separate and cross. So each side of the brain sees with halves of both eyes!

EYES LEFT, RIGHT

Six long, slim muscles pull on the eyeball to make it look around.

Eye-moving muscle

EXTRA LENSES

If the eye's own lens is too strong or not strong enough, this can blur vision. Glass or plastic lenses, in eyeglasses or as contact lenses, make vision clear again.

Contact lenses

SPARE-PART SURGERY

Ophthalmic (eye) surgeons can put artificial lenses into the eye, if the natural lens becomes cloudy as in cataract. Or they can shave pieces off the cornea with a laser beam, to cure short or long sightedness.

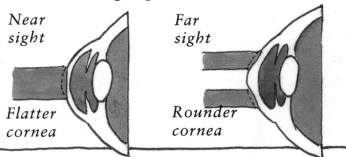

Near sight

Far sight

Flatter cornea

Rounder cornea

THE LISTENING BRAIN

Ears do what eyes do – inform the brain about the world around. But they do it with sound, rather than light. Ears hear deep roars, high squeals, the wind rustling the leaves, and the latest and loudest disco music. They send all this information to the brain. The brain chooses what it wants to hear.

LOUD PAIN

The brain knows when something is so loud that it might damage the delicate inner ear. It feels "painfully loud." Listen to what the brain says, and care for hearing.

EAR TRUMPET

The outer ear is simply a flap of skin and cartilage (gristle). It does not hear. It collects sound waves and funnels them into the ear canal.

LOW AND HIGH

The highness of a sound is measured in Hertz, Hz. Our ears detect rumbles as low as 100 Hz, and squeaks as high as 10,000 Hz. But the bat has us beaten. It hears its own squeaks at 200,000 Hz.

SPIES ON YOUR INSIDES

With a flashlight-like otoscope, the doctor can see deep into the ear. (Or, if no brain, right through!)

SPARE-PART SURGERY

People who are hard of hearing can use an ear trumpet to help collect more sound. ENT (ear, nose and throat) surgeons may replace a diseased tiny stirrup ear bone with a plastic one.

Hearing aid

Plastic ear bone

EARS AND EYES
The inner parts of the ear, which do the actual hearing, are protected deep in the skull bone, just behind the eyes.

FALLING OVER
In each ear are three fluid-filled, semicircular canals. Part of the balance system, they detect head movements.

Semi-circular canals

Skull bone

Air space of middle ear cavity

TO THE BRAIN
Signals go to the brain along the auditory nerve.

Ear canal

Anvil

Stirrup

Hammer

BOOM BOOM
At the end of the ear canal is the eardrum, a taut piece of thin skin the size of a fingernail. Sound waves make it vibrate. If ear wax in the canal builds up and stops the eardrum from moving freely, the doctor can squirt it away with a jet of water.

EAR BONES
Sound vibrations rattle the eardrum at the end of the ear canal. The eardrum is joined to the first of three tiny bones in the middle ear cavity. Vibrations pass along these bones to the cochlea.

HERE WE HEAR
The snail-like cochlea is the heart of hearing. Sound vibrations pass from the ear bones to the fluid inside the cochlea. The vibrations rock microscopic hairs, and these movements generate patterns of nerve signals.

Eustachian tube to throat

Magnified view of hairs in cochlea

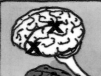

TASTE'N'SNIFF WHIFFS

We usually do not realize, but the brain checks all food and drink going into the body. Occasionally food is extra-yummy and we say "Delicious!" Rarely it is truly yukky and we say "Horrible!" Smell and taste save us from eating foods that have gone rotten, or that are somehow bad.

SMELL THAT TASTE!

Taste and smell are separate senses. But when we eat, our minds are used to a combination of flavors and odors. If the nose is blocked, foods "taste" strangely boring, since we lack smell.

TIP OF THE TONGUE
The tongue is the body's most mobile, flexible muscle. The brain can instruct it to shift food around for chewing, and bend into all manner of shapes for speaking and whistling. (And poke out of the mouth.)

Papillae (lumps) on tongue surface

SEM
A scanning electron microscope displays real-looking, 3-D tongue papillae.

SPIES ON YOUR INSIDES

One of the most fascinating methods of looking at the body is through a microscope. Usually, tiny bits are removed from the body and stained (dyed) so they show up clearly under the microscope. Doctors can see individual cells, and detect disease early.

LIGHT MICROSCOPE
Individual cells in a taste bud show up under the light microscope.

Onion-shaped cell cluster

Sensory hair

Papilla

Taste buds

UP THE NOSE

Inside the nose is a large chamber, the nasal cavity. In its roof is a patch of frilly hairs, the olfactory epithelium. These hairs detect odors.

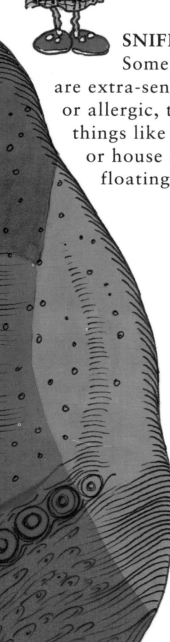

Olfactory bulb and nerve to brain

Skull bone

Olfactory epithelium

Nasal cavity

SNIFF-SNEEZE

Some noses are extra-sensitive, or allergic, to things like pollen or house dust floating in the air.

Nostril

Branches of lingual nerve inside tongue

Base of tongue

COLORS

Blue: sweet and salty
Red: bitter
Orange: sour
Purple: not a lot

THE TASTE AREAS

Different parts of the tongue are most sensitive to certain basic flavors. But the brain probably decides on the taste from the overall pattern of nerve signals from the taste buds.

PLENTY OF NERVE

The tongue is mostly muscle. But is also has the usual blood supply, and plenty of nerves. Most of these are lingual branches of the face nerves. They carry nerve signals from the 8,000 microscopic taste buds scattered on the tongue's surface.

A TOUCHY BRAIN

Strange thing, but the brain has no feelings. It is not sensitive to touch. Brain surgeons can poke and prod it, and the person would not feel a thing. For information about what is touching the body, and whether it is hard or soft, hot or cold, dry or slimy, the brain relies on the skin.

AT OUR FINGERTIPS

Microsensors are dotted by their millions in the skin. They are especially common in the fingertips, where they detect the slightest touch.

GUILTY!
Each finger of every person has a unique fingerprint. Which is why fingerprints are used to catch criminals.

TOUCH 2
Micro-sensors called Ruffini's receptors are on the lookout for hot things.

Fingernail

TOUCH BY NUMBERS
Microscopic view:

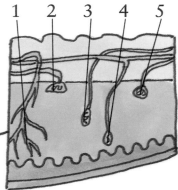

1 2 3 4 5

Finger bone

TOUCH 1
Free nerve endings sense pain, and warn the brain to move the skin at once.

TOUCH 3
Krause's receptors tend to tell the brain about very cold things.

TOUCH 4
Meissner's receptors feel light pressure and soft, delicate touches.

TOUCH 5
Pacinian receptors are ready to tell the brain about hard-pressed skin.

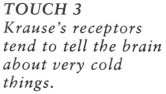

CHAPTER FIVE

The BRAIN *in* CONTROL

Walk forward. Stop. Touch the floor. Jump up. Laugh loudly, ha-ha! The brain has great fun ordering muscles to pull on bones, and make the body do whatever it wants.

THE BRAIN'S BONES

Bones are tough. Bones are strong. Bones are hard, and white. Some people say bones are boring. But bones are not. They are as alive and as exciting as any other part of the body. Bones surround and protect the brain, and form a jointed framework that holds up the entire body.

SPARE-PART SURGERY

Bones are the business of orthopedic surgeons, who specialize in muscles, bones and joints. If a bone cracks or snaps, it can be strengthened by a plate or strip, made of metal or plastic. This is screwed or glued to the bone fragments while they heal together. Some bones can be replaced by artificial versions.

SPIES ON YOUR INSIDES

Bones show up clearly as white shapes on X-rays. So do the metal plates, pins and screws that fix broken bones.

Pin

STRONG BONES

Bones are made of minerals such as calcium. Foods such as milk are, too. They help bone health.

COMPACT BONE
Bones are not solid and the same all the way through. They would be far too heavy. Their main strength comes from the hard, dense substance called compact bone, which forms a strong outer shell for each bone.

Shaft

Neck

Head

SPONGY BONE
Where great strength is not quite so vital, bone has a spongy or honeycomb structure. This reduces weight and also saves on valuable bone-building minerals.

Shell of hard bone

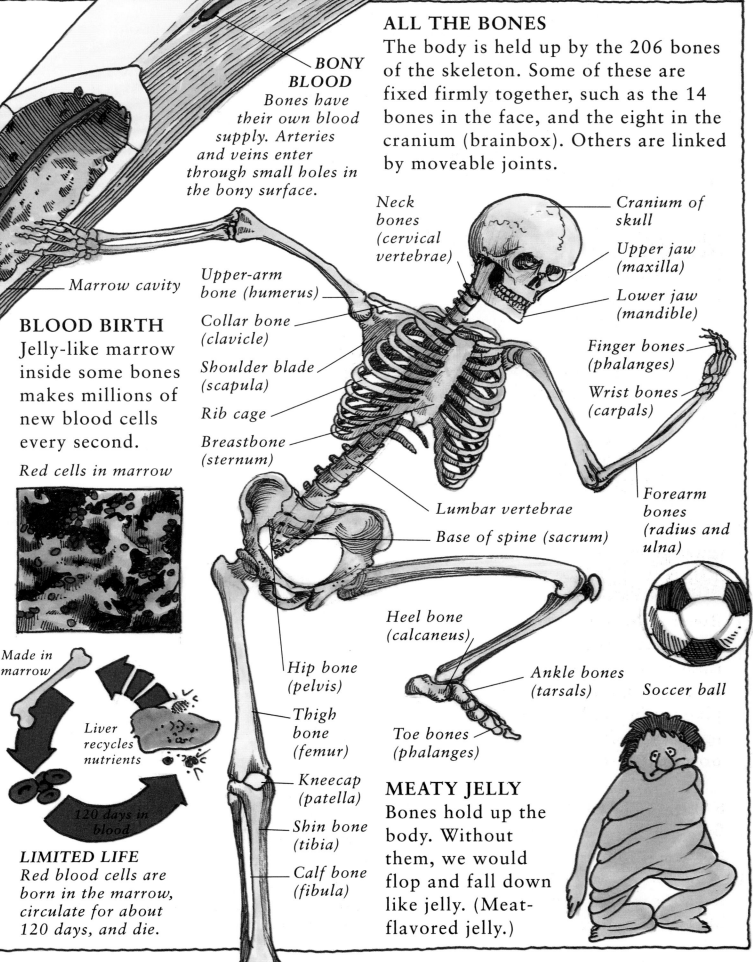

BONY BLOOD
Bones have their own blood supply. Arteries and veins enter through small holes in the bony surface.

ALL THE BONES
The body is held up by the 206 bones of the skeleton. Some of these are fixed firmly together, such as the 14 bones in the face, and the eight in the cranium (brainbox). Others are linked by moveable joints.

Marrow cavity

BLOOD BIRTH
Jelly-like marrow inside some bones makes millions of new blood cells every second.

Red cells in marrow

Made in marrow

Liver recycles nutrients

120 days in blood

LIMITED LIFE
Red blood cells are born in the marrow, circulate for about 120 days, and die.

Neck bones (cervical vertebrae)

Cranium of skull

Upper jaw (maxilla)

Lower jaw (mandible)

Upper-arm bone (humerus)

Collar bone (clavicle)

Shoulder blade (scapula)

Rib cage

Breastbone (sternum)

Finger bones (phalanges)

Wrist bones (carpals)

Forearm bones (radius and ulna)

Lumbar vertebrae

Base of spine (sacrum)

Hip bone (pelvis)

Thigh bone (femur)

Kneecap (patella)

Shin bone (tibia)

Calf bone (fibula)

Heel bone (calcaneus)

Ankle bones (tarsals)

Toe bones (phalanges)

Soccer ball

MEATY JELLY
Bones hold up the body. Without them, we would flop and fall down like jelly. (Meat-flavored jelly.)

JOINING BONES

If bones were not joined together, where would we be? In a stiff heap on the floor. Bones may be strong and rigid. But joints make the body flexible and mobile, so that we can walk and run, jump and bend, and play computer games.

CAREFULLY DOES IT!

Joints have a lot of wear and sometimes tear. Even the fittest and best-trained athletes sometimes sprain or dislocate ("put out") a joint. Gentle bending and warm-up exercises help

to prepare the joints, muscles and body – and the mind – for the contest ahead.

THE KNEE
This is the body's largest single joint. It has two crescent-shaped pieces of cartilage, the menisci, for extra stability.

SPIES ON YOUR INSIDES

The orthopedic surgeon looks inside a large joint, such as the knee, through a small slit, with a telescope-like arthroscope. Better than cutting it all open!

DOWN TO THE TIPPY-TOES
The toes have tiny joints, right down to their last bones. The joints may be small, but they have all the cartilages and other bits of the bigger joints.

Rounded end of thigh bone

Bone knuckle (condyle)

C-shaped menisci

Ligament

Calf bone

Shin bone

Base of shin bone (tibia)

Small sliding movements in several directions

Ankle bone (talus)

SLIDE, SLIDE
The main ankle joint is of the sliding type. The topmost ankle bone can slide around slightly under the base of the shin bone.

HINGE, HINGE
The knee is a good example of the hinge joint. It allows movement in only one direction. The lower leg can swing to the rear, but not to the sides or front. The kneecap protects and strengthens the front of the joint.

Thigh bone (femur)

Kneecap

Shin bone (tibia)

Swinging hinge movement in one direction

Calf bone (fibula)

SPARE-PART SURGERY
There are many different plastic and metal artificial joints. They replace real joints which have suffered from arthritis or other conditions, and are painful and stiff. Hips and knuckles are the joints most often replaced.

BALL, SOCKET
The hip has the ball and socket design. This gives great mobility, with the leg moving in almost any direction. The shoulder is a similar design and is even more flexible.

Socket in hip bone (pelvis)

Ball-shaped head of thigh bone (femur)

Swiveling movements in many directions

Shaft of thigh bone

MUSCLES

By itself, the brain cannot move. But it has plenty of muscle at its command, to make movements for it. In fact, there are nearly 640 muscles. They pull on bones and move the head and body.

Muscle narrows into tendon

Muscle sheath (epimysium)

Bundle of myofibers

Myofiber

Myofibrils

INSIDE A MUSCLE

The bulging part of a muscle is made of small stringy bits, myofibers. These are made of even smaller stringy bits, myofibrils. These are the parts that get shorter, or contract.

Tendons pull finger bones

ON THE BONE

Few muscles join directly to bones. They narrow into rope-like tendons that attach to bones. Tendons in the hand are long and slim.

Finger-moving muscles in forearm

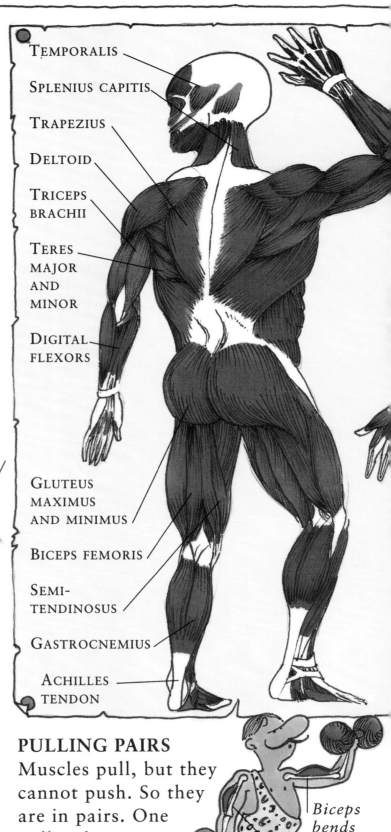

- TEMPORALIS
- SPLENIUS CAPITIS
- TRAPEZIUS
- DELTOID
- TRICEPS BRACHII
- TERES MAJOR AND MINOR
- DIGITAL FLEXORS
- GLUTEUS MAXIMUS AND MINIMUS
- BICEPS FEMORIS
- SEMI-TENDINOSUS
- GASTROCNEMIUS
- ACHILLES TENDON

PULLING PAIRS

Muscles pull, but they cannot push. So they are in pairs. One pulls a bone one way. The partner pulls it back again.

Biceps bends elbow

Triceps pulls it back

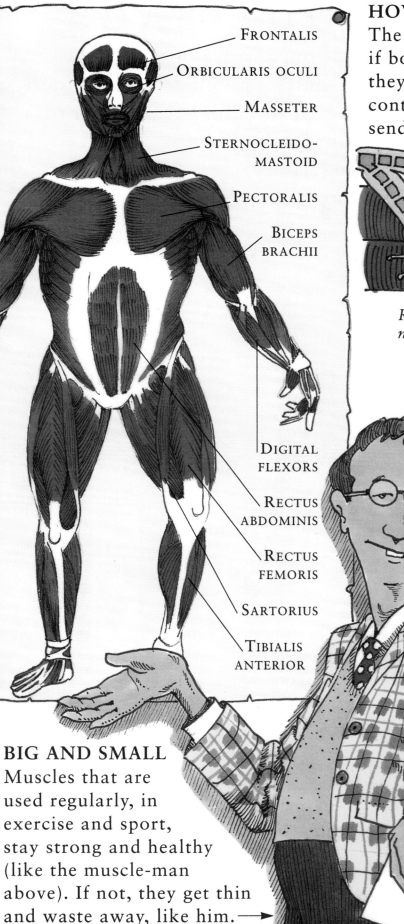

FRONTALIS

ORBICULARIS OCULI

MASSETER

STERNOCLEIDO-
MASTOID

PECTORALIS

BICEPS
BRACHII

DIGITAL
FLEXORS

RECTUS
ABDOMINIS

RECTUS
FEMORIS

SARTORIUS

TIBIALIS
ANTERIOR

HOW MUSCLES SHORTEN

The brain would hardly be in control if body muscles shortened whenever they wished. So it has them under the control of nerve signals, which it sends along motor nerves.

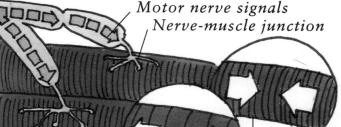

Motor nerve signals
Nerve-muscle junction

Relaxed muscle

Contracted muscle

SPARE-PART SURGERY

Some muscles are less important than others. So surgeons can move muscles or pieces of them, to replace muscles that are diseased or injured. They move the muscle from a place where it will hardly be missed, to a place where it is needed more. This is very helpful for small hand muscles.

Moved bottom muscle needs control!

BIG AND SMALL

Muscles that are used regularly, in exercise and sport, stay strong and healthy (like the muscle-man above). If not, they get thin and waste away, like him. →

BRAIN'S BODY-BAG

Skin, as the song says, keeps our insides in. Skin also keeps the outsides out. The outsides include dirt and dust, germs, bumps and scrapes, too much heat or cold, harmful sun rays, and the drying effects of wind and sun. So the brain is very thankful to the skin for this wonderful protection, as well as for providing the sense of touch (page 48).

Sweat pore

Sweat gland

DEAD OR ALIVE

Look at a body. Almost all of what we see is dead. The outer surface of skin is made of cells that died days ago, as described opposite. The surface gets worn away and continually renews itself. It changes color, too. If the body goes out in strong sunlight, skin darkens to protect it from the sun's harmful ultraviolet rays.

BIG SKIN

Skin is the largest organ (main part). Unzipped, it would weigh over eight pounds.

INSIDE SKIN

Under a microscope, we can see that skin has sweat glands, hairs, and millions of other amazing parts.

2 square yards of best skin, going cheap

HAIR-PIT
There are about five million hairs on an average body. Most are too small to see easily. They grow from pits called hair follicles.

UNDER-SKIN FAT
A soft blanket of fat, the subcutaneous layer, protects and cushions the parts below.

SKIN SACRIFICE

The top millimeter or less of skin is called the epidermis. Its basal cells are busy multiplying by the million daily. They move upward, fill with the tough substance keratin, die, and reach the surface, ready to be rubbed and worn away.

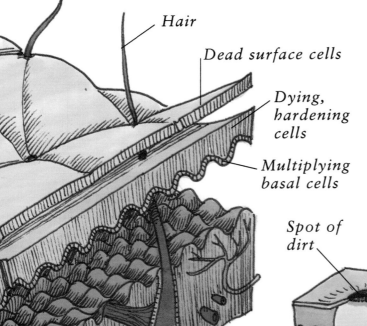

Hair

Dead surface cells

Dying, hardening cells

Multiplying basal cells

Spot of dirt

Hair follicle

LONG AND LONG

Nails are made from keratin, the same toughening substance in skin and hair. People grow their hair and nails long for many reasons, such as religion, or vanity. The longest nail ever was a thumbnail, at 46 inches. The longest hair was over 236 inches.

IN-SKIN BLEMISHES

Sometimes a hair follicle gets blocked by dirt or the skin's natural oils. Regular washing helps clean skin.

Pimple

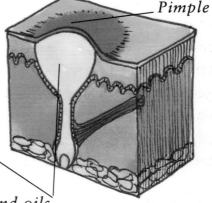

Build-up of natural skin waxes and oils

THE UNDER-SKIN

Under the epidermis layer is the dermis. It contains touch sensors, blood vessels, and strong fibers of keratin and elastin. The dermis is usually thicker than the epidermis, except on wear-and-tear surfaces such as the soles and palms.

COOL AND DAMP

About three million sweat glands are scattered in the skin. When the body is too hot, they release watery sweat onto the surface. As it dries, it cools.

SPARE-PART SURGERY

In an accident, skin is the first part to get cut, burned or injured. Skin experts called dermatologists* can sometimes mend the damage with skin from other body parts, with artificial skin, or temporarily with skin from pigs.

* Some skin experts are called Mike or Tina.

BABY BRAINS

The brain's way of producing more brains is to get its body to make babies. Each baby grows and grows, and develops its own brain – plus a complete body to go with it. The process of making babies differs greatly, depending on whether the brain's body is female or male.

GETTING TOGETHER

A baby starts as two microscopic cells. One is an egg from the mother, smaller than this dot >. The other is a sperm from the father, even smaller and shaped like a tadpole. The two are brought together by sexual intercourse (a term often shortened to "sex" when people are in a hurry).

Sperm cell
Egg cell

LIFE CYCLE

Egg and sperm join together and start their growth and development. It is a long journey. About 20 years later the body is grown up.

Sperm and egg join
Cells multiply to 2, 4, 8 and so on

MOTHER
The baby grows for nine months in the womb, or uterus, inside its mother's body. It is dark and cramped in the womb. But on birthday, the wide world is very bright and noisy.

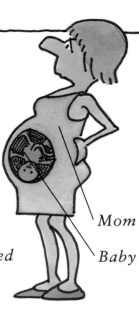
Mom
Baby

SPIES ON YOUR INSIDES

The ultrasound scanner uses high-pitched sound waves, too high for us to hear. It beams them harmlessly into the womb, detects the echoes, and displays them as a picture of the growing baby.

MINUS 8 MONTHS
The baby has the beginnings of a head and eyes, and its heart is beating. But there are no proper arms or legs.

MINUS 7 MONTHS
The baby is only as big as a thumb. Yet all of its main body parts have formed, even its miniature fingers and toes.

Tiny brain
Bigger brain

SPARE-PART SURGERY

Body chemicals called hormones travel around in the blood and control many inner processes. For example, growth is controlled by growth hormone. Scientists can now make growth hormone by genetic engineering. The amounts they give must also be controlled!

Practicality of middle age

Wisdom of mature years

Enthusiasm of youth

GROWING UP
As the physical body grows, it follows a fairly set pattern. As the mind develops in its brain, it learns knowledge, gathers experiences, and – if we are lucky – accumulates wisdom.

LIFELINE
During womb life, the umbilical cord carries nutrients and oxygen from the mother to her baby.

The main structure of the brain is well formed

Brain nearly grown

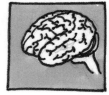

Brain volume tends to shrink in later years

Brain becomes more bulging

MINUS 3 MONTHS
Six months after it started to grow, the baby floats in a pool of fluid inside its mother's womb.

ZERO (BIRTHDAY)
The baby's brain is more than three-quarters grown. Yet its body will become 20 times bigger as it grows to adulthood.

PLUS 1 YEAR
The baby's brain is learning astonishing feats – how to walk and talk, and how to hold things and throw them across the room. Years later, all this will be so easy.

AND THE REST
The brain learns incredible amounts of knowledge – more than 10 new words every day during the school years. During the later years, the memory may begin to forget recent events.

GLOSSARY

Antibody A chemical made by white cells in the blood, that kills or disables germs which have invaded the body.

Artery A blood vessel that carries blood away from the heart. (Not all arteries contain red, high-oxygen blood. The pulmonary arteries which go to the lungs carry blue, low-oxygen blood.)

Bone A strong, stiff body part that holds up all the other soft, squishy parts. The body has 206 individual bones. They are made chiefly of the substance collagen, plus crystals of minerals such as calcium and phosphorus.

Cartilage "Gristle," a slightly soft, pearly-white body substance. It forms the framework of parts such as the nose, ear and the voicebox (larynx). It also lines the ends of bones where they move against each other in a joint.

Cell A microscopic unit of life, from which all living things are made. The human body contains billions of cells, of hundreds of different kinds, such as nerve cells, muscle cells, blood cells and so on.

Cerebral hemisphere
Half of the large, dome-shaped upper part of the brain.

Cortex The gray, bulging, wrinkled outer surface of the cerebral hemispheres of the brain.

Cranial nerve A nerve that joins directly to the brain, rather than to the spinal cord.

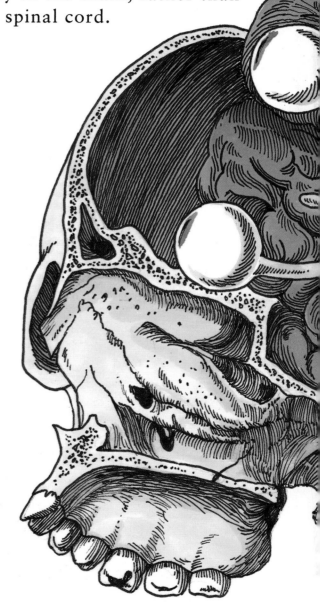

Gland A part that makes a substance for use in the body. Salivary glands make saliva, the watery "spit" that we chew into our food to make it soft and swallow-able.

Hormone A body chemical made in a gland called an endocrine gland. It controls the activities of certain body parts, called its target organs.

Muscle A body part specialized to get shorter, or contract, and move whatever it is joined to. Many organs have their own muscle, such as the heart and intestines. But when we say "a muscle" we usually mean one of the skeletal muscles that pulls on a bone of the skeleton.

Nerve A long, thin body part specialized for carrying information, in the form of tiny electrical signals.

Organ A major body part, such as the heart, liver, kidney – and of course, the brain.

Sensory nerve A nerve that transmits sensory nerve signals, from the sense organs (eyes, ears and so on) to the brain, telling it about the world around.

System In the body, several organs and other parts that work together to carry out one major function. For example, the mouth, teeth, gullet, stomach, intestines and liver form the digestive system, which gets nourishment into the body.

Motor nerve A nerve that transmits motor nerve signals, from the brain to the muscles, telling them to contract.

Vein A blood vessel that carries blood back to the heart. (Not all veins contain blue, low-oxygen blood. The pulmonary veins from the lungs carry red, high-oxygen blood.)

X-ray A type of invisible ray that has great penetrating power. This means it can pass through soft body tissues such as muscles and intestines. However it cannot pass through hard, dense substances such as bones, so these show up white on a radiograph (an X-ray photograph).

INDEX